CROSSWINDS

poems by

Debbie Richard

Finishing Line Press
Georgetown, Kentucky

CROSSWINDS

Copyright © 2021 by Debbie Richard
ISBN 978-1-64662-700-4 First Edition
All rights reserved under International and Pan-American Copyright Conventions. No part of this book may be reproduced in any manner whatsoever without written permission from the publisher, except in the case of brief quotations embodied in critical articles and reviews.

ACKNOWLEDGMENTS

Grateful acknowledgment to the editors of the following publications in which these poems have appeared:

"Unveiling;" "Memorialized;" "Evanesce;" "Firsts"—*Literature for the People* (Malta, UK)
"First Time in New York"—*Adelaide Literary Award Anthology*; Finalist for Best Poem 2019—Adelaide Books, New York
"Rapunzel"—*Adelaide Literary Award Anthology*; Short-listed for Best Poem 2018—Adelaide Books, New York
"Sunday Afternoon at the Park"—*WestWard Quarterly*
"Crawdad"—*Mountain Ink*
"Laid Open"—*Women Speak* (Women of Appalachia Project Anthology)
"Rebirth;" "Dayspring"—*Founder's Favourites* (Canada)
"Vacuum"—*Elk River Living Magazine*

Publisher: Leah Huete de Maines
Editor: Christen Kincaid
Cover Art: Asuka Ng, www.Askas-Atelier.com
Author Photo: Deborah E. Simmons
Cover Design: Elizabeth Maines McCleavy

Order online: www.finishinglinepress.com
also available on amazon.com

Author inquiries and mail orders:
Finishing Line Press
PO Box 1626
Georgetown, Kentucky 40324
USA

Table of Contents

Unveiling 1

First Time in New York 2

Rapunzel 3

Sunday Afternoon at the Park 4

Crawdad 5

Tranquil 6

Firsts 7

Memorialized 8

Sunflowers 9

Junkie 10

Evanesce 11

Haven 12

Disguise 13

The High Meadow 14

Laid Open 15

Rebirth 16

I Listen for You 17

Dayspring 18

Vacuum 19

A Measure of Grace 20

Unveiling

The sweet confection
tucked inside
the smooth white
parchment paper,
The rustling of the tiny package
between my fingers
as anticipation mounts
with the unveiling of
coarse, chocolate swirls
atop a truffle center,
unexpected,
yet pleasing to the touch,
the taste.

Pleasing as the sweet kiss
of a young bride for her groom,
as he unwraps
her white crinkled
taffeta gown,
his hands roving over
her tawny skin,
devouring
each sweet, delectable
sensation inside.

First Time in New York

Tall steel buildings in Manhattan,
flanked with windows, loomed over us
as we attempted to keep up with the crowd
bustling through the streets.

Yellow taxi cabs vied for our fare,
their driving causing us to gasp
as they madly darted in and out of traffic.

Some streets were lined with garbage,
contrasting with the pristine golden clad frontage
of the Waldorf Astoria, or Fifth Avenue's
enchanting window displays.

Brightly lit marquees displaying morning news
personalities, live music and shows,
along with the latest fashions,
added to the appeal of Times Square.

Brooklyn Bridge's multiple cables were
draped like string on a model ship,
twinkling at night, adding to the magic of the city.

Yet among all the steel, and glass, and noise
is an oasis, Central Park—
fresh and green, awaiting those who jog,
or picnic, or perhaps just relax under a tree
with a good book.

Rapunzel

Her prison was not a round brick tower
like the one in the fairy-tale,
but a bedroom in the upstairs of a house
where a window overlooked the grounds—
green, lush, inviting.
A Tyrant, no less, oversaw her existence
with rarely a word of kindness,
most often sharply spoken words
meant to keep her oppressed.
This maiden's blond hair, too, had
been cut short, leaving her without
a means of escape.

Sunday Afternoon at the Park

As I sit on this park bench, watching the ripples
on a lazy river and listening to the sounds
of a Sunday afternoon—the thump, thump, thump
of a basketball as a father plays with his children,
an excited cry from a child, two boys racing to climb trees
side by side, the breeze gently lifting the pages of a book
I hold in my lap—the story of a young Amish woman
who just lost her husband and son to a tragic accident.

Such contrast from what I observe today—
A young couple walking their dog on the circular trail,
a covey of birds flitting over the water with the sunshine
warm upon their wings, two girls passing by on the trail
chatting away as one pushes a stroller, oblivious to my
intense gaze at the baby who has been all but forgotten.

Across from the basketball court, little boys play on
the green slide, the smallest crawling up the front to slide
back down again, then transferring their attention
to the monkey bars where their older brother swings,
competition at an early age—

A father and daughter sit in the shade after a few rounds of basketball,
the American flag waves proudly beneath a powder blue sky with
pronounced clouds, some appearing to have been airbrushed,
while others resemble cotton candy, stretched at the corners
to form various shapes, and gliding midair as if trying to connect
with others, while sunlight peeks through, giving a slightly gray hue,
as if a shaded effect had been added.

As families leave, the quiet descends once again—
the gentle breeze, the cry of a bird in a nearby tree,
the sunshine and shade of the mature trees spilling
across the grass, a few fallen leaves lie crumpled on the ground,
a hint of Fall is in the air, a beautiful day indeed
before the cold winds of winter descend.

Crawdad

The blue crawdad, its pinchers flailing,
crawled out of its hideout in the damp earth,
a hole in my Grandmother's yard.
He seemed to be out of place,
this granddaddy of all crawdads,
royal in color and size,
larger than the small brown ones
we usually saw while playing
in the nearby creek.
His features resembled that of a small lobster,
colored differently, blue instead of red,
as our blood appears
when it comes to the surface.

Tranquil

The early morning is still,
hushed, as if a TV was muted.
The white cat is stretched out on my desk,
her underbelly cool from the glass top,
restful, sensing this is the peaceful time of day.
My husband hasn't awakened yet.
The phones haven't started
their incessant ringing,
when clients call,
pouring out their distresses,
afflictions troubling *their* lives.
Once they retain my husband,
he assumes his role as advocate,
launching an investigation,
pleading their cause,
calming their fears.

Evening comes, the phones stop ringing,
but where is the quiet, the calm?
The white cat is under the bed,
waiting for morning, when stillness returns.

Firsts

When I splashed through the creek for the first time
    below my Grandma's house and saw
    minnows swimming in the shallow water,
    darting in and out between the rocks,
    I wanted to see what secret places
    the minnows saw that I couldn't, so hiking up
    my dress tail, I stepped across the slippery rocks,
    teetering from one to another
    as if in a game of Hopscotch.

The first day in the two-room schoolhouse
    in the curve of the road, nestled between the creek
    on one side and a steep hill on the other,
    a little blond-haired girl scolded me
    for taking her seat. Did she know
    her sense of place at such an early age?

The first time we plucked daisies to see if
    "He loves me or if he loves me not,"
    the delicate white petals drifted towards the ground
    like destined thoughts scattered in the wind.

The first time I kissed a boy was in the churchyard
    after service one Sunday night, looking into the twinkling
    eyes of the boy with light brown curls,
    the one someone said I was "robbing the cradle" with.

The first time I wished upon a falling star,
    I kept the wish to myself
    hoping it might actually come true,
    or perhaps, because it was something
    I couldn't possibly let anyone else know about.

Memorialized

Driving to the store to buy flowers
on the Friday before Memorial Day,
a wave of grief gripped me until I
could barely breathe.

Trying desperately to fight back the tears,
my throat constricted until the emotional pain
evolved into physical pain.

While other families are planning trips to
the beach or the mountains,
cookouts or bonfires,
my weekend will be tinged with
a mixture of sadness and memories
as I visit my family at the cemetery.

Yet, I'm grateful I had these people in my life
as long as I did… remembering
my mother's gentle touch, my dad's strength,
my brother's teasing way, my grandmothers
making me feel loved and cherished.

They are at rest now, and I have the eternal
promise of seeing them again one day.
I hope they would have been proud of the
woman I've become.

Sunflowers

Huge
brown
eyes
with
smiles
reaching
toward
the
light.

Junkie

I stealthily creep into the kitchen
to determine what is making
that crunching sound.
I spy him—perched on the top shelf
of the baker's rack
with a bag of Doritos by his side,
chips between his claws, those same
sharp claws, which in one swift *pop*
burst the snack bag open—
like the hit and crash of a pair of cymbals.
The possum, with his long snout and beady eyes,
glares back at me as if to say,
You want some?

Evanesce

The Spring snow comes twirling,
whirling past the windowpane,
diagonally, like sheets of rain
on a slanted roof. Individual flakes
dart through the air like popcorn
in a hot oiled machine, with mounting
speed as if in a hurry to reach
their destination, only to dissipate
like vapor in the warmth of the sun's
rays, similar to how one might feel
in the arms of their truelove.

Haven

A lonesome hearth,
a dying fire,
embers sinking low—
In an easy chair,
a father sits
and tells stories of long ago.
A howling wind
whistles fierce
and rattles window panes—
A candle flickers
and slowly dies
as the storm brings pelting rain.
A sleepy child
nestles close
within his father's arm—
Inside this house,
though the tempests blow,
they're sheltered from the storm.

Disguise
> *(for Arlis D. Richard, in memoriam)*

As a little girl, I was naïve enough to believe
there would always be a strong man looking out for me.
A father figure who wore navy blue work pants,
brown boots with rawhide ties, and carried a silver
lunch pail to work. This rugged man would fight all my battles,
scare away the monsters lurking in the shadows
and haunting my dreams.

In my early teens, he took on another image,
with bloodshot eyes and a fierce temper.
He became the one we fled from.
For you see, the whiskey possessed him and he
became someone I no longer recognized, the one who
now haunted my dreams.

After what seemed like an eternity, he gave up the liquor
and his demeanor changed. He became the calm,
wise, and supportive man I had once known. But eventually,
he had a monster of his own to battle—Cancer.
Worse than the fiery liquid which once passed his lips
and settled into his soul, leaving him empty, hollow, when
the effects wore off. Cancer didn't relent;
it ravaged his body, as a bleak outcome
haunted his dreams.

This giant of a man has passed on now, like so many of our
mountain folk. He made peace with his Maker,
peace with his family. A legacy of love and strength lives on.
No more haunts in our dreams.

The High Meadow

We round the curve in this old dirt road
where we've walked so many summers before,
picking blackberries from tangled vines,
the sweet dark juice running down our chins.

At the top of the hill, tall grass
and prickly wildflowers
all but hide two young deer
romping at the edge of the clearing.

We take cover in the green sanctuary,
but sensing our approach,
they snort, then disappear
into the coolness of the deep woods.

Laid Open

I stare at the nearly empty egg carton on the counter,
gray with corrugated edges, rough grooves on the outside,
strong enough to protect the lone egg inside—
white, oval, smooth, supported by barriers
encompassing something so delicate, so fragile.
When the lid is closed, the egg is tucked
away in a cool, safe place.

I often feel loneliness, as if I am the only one
existing in a harsh world, laid open—a rough exterior
towering over me, attempting to break my shell,
my will to survive. I huddle alone in my room
with the door barred, and wish I could crawl
into that carton with the egg, pull the lid down over me,
hide away in a safe place.

Rebirth
(Haiku)

Waterfalls cascade.
Wise men cleanse impurities,
Trespasses submerged.

I Listen for You

I listen for you, even after you've gone.
As I close my eyes, I still feel the whisper
of your breath on my neck, calling my name softly
You swallow—gulping, greedily
as if your very existence hinges on my existence.
Tantalizing, you seek my mouth,
Teasingly, you back away, but then come closer
as the tip of your tongue licks my bottom lip
and trails to the tip of my nose
You part my lips. As your tongue thrusts deep inside
you breathe heat into my soul
as our limbs entwine and we become one.

Dayspring

To never tire of the crashing waves
upon the distant shore,
or watch the great ball of fire
arise from a blue abyss
like a tangled web of seaweed
pulls creatures from the ocean floor.
Look skyward toward the heavenly light
and be clothed in the warmth of nature's kiss.

Vacuum

Empty space—is that all we are?
Protecting ourselves from outside influences?
Life is a balance—suctioning in the pure,
while purging the filth,
for a desert is a dry, lonely place.

A Measure of Grace

Grace is more than a few words spoken over a meal.
Grace is a virtue coming from God,
pardon, undeserved favor.

Grace is an act of kindness,
a courtesy, as when someone holds the door open for you
or shares their umbrella in a downpour.

Graceful beauty appears effortless,
as butterflies flitting over a field of wildflowers
or the elegance of a ballerina gliding across a stage.

Grace gives meaning to our lives,
renewed hope in an otherwise hopeless world
where pandemics and fear dare to dictate
every detail of our lives, as if we were trapped
in a huge bubble, cut off from the outside world.

But I would choose to be inside a *snow globe*
where Christmas comes every day of the year.

Debbie Richard was born in Parkersburg, WV. She graduated from West Virginia Career College with honors in 1987 and moved to South Carolina three years later, following her love of the ocean. Debbie started writing seriously in 2009 while full-time caregiver for her mother. Watching her mother's failing health between 2009 and her passing in 2011, Debbie found writing a means of healing. She hopes her writing will cause others to feel something, to move them in some way.

Debbie is listed in the *Directory of Poets & Writers* as both a poet and creative nonfiction writer. She is a member of South Carolina Writers Association and West Virginia Writers Inc. She was short-listed for Best Poem in *Adelaide Literary Award for Poetry, 2018*. Her poems have appeared in various magazines and journals including *Torrid Literature Journal, Adelaide Literary Magazine, Literature for the People, WestWard Quarterly, Halcyon Days*, and others.

Resiliency, a chapbook of poetry, was published in 2012 by Finishing Line Press. *Hills of Home*, an Appalachian memoir, was released in 2014 by eLectio Publishing. An Audio book of Hills of Home was released in 2018 by Sweetsong Productions and is available on Audible. *PIVOT*, an illustrated volume of poetry, was released in January 2019 by Adelaide Books of New York. *PIVOT* received an Honorable Mention in the 2019 New York Book Festival Awards, and was reviewed by Readers' Favorite, receiving a 5-star review.

Debbie spends time between her home state of West Virginia and the beautiful coast of South Carolina. Find her online at www.debbierichard.com

www.ingramcontent.com/pod-product-compliance
Lightning Source LLC
LaVergne TN
LVHW041525070426
835507LV00013B/1825